Top 10 Worst

Spooky Mysteries

you wouldn't want to know about!

Gareth Stevens
Publishing

Please visit our Web site, **www.garethstevens.com**. For a free color catalog of all our high-quality books, call toll free 1-800-542-2595 or fax 1-877-542-2596.

Library of Congress Cataloging-in-Publication Data

Macdonald, Fiona, 1958-
Spooky mysteries / Fiona Macdonald.
    p. cm. — (Top ten worst)
Includes index.
ISBN 978-1-4339-4071-2 (pbk.)
ISBN 978-1-4339-4072-9 (6-pack)
ISBN 978-1-4339-4070-5 (library binding)
1. Curiosities and wonders. I. Title.
AG243.M27 2011
001.94—dc22
                                    2010007392

First Edition

Published in 2011 by
Gareth Stevens Publishing
111 East 14th Street, Suite 349
New York, NY 10003

© 2010 The Salariya Book Company Ltd

Series creator: David Salariya
Editor: Jamie Pitman
Illustrations by David Antram

Printed in Heshan, China

CPSIA compliance information: Batch #SS10GS: For further information contact Gareth Stevens, New York, New York at 1-800-542-2595.

Top 10 Worst™

Spooky Mysteries

you wouldn't want to know about!

Illustrated by
David Antram

Written by
fiona Macdonald

Created & designed by
David Salariya

Contents

Into the unknown!

L et this book lead you on a strange, scary journey— into the unknown! That's a place full of mystery, half-truths, and confusion. You will find that some mysteries have a simple, sensible explanation—but that others cannot be explained, and still trouble us…

It might not be a good idea to read this book at bedtime!

Tremble

Shudder

Zzzzzz

Stretch your mind!

Most of us enjoy a good mystery story. We like to learn strange facts, and puzzle over peculiar happenings. It's exciting to discover how much we don't know or can't understand. Mysteries challenge us to think. They stretch our minds!

Why do we like mysteries?

Loch Ness monster

They scare us (but not too much).

They help us understand.

They're good old stories.

They help us face our fears.

They make us wonder.

Yeti

They excite our imagination.

They tell us about the world and its wonders.

They entertain us.

They puzzle us.

Ha ha!!

They make us laugh (or cry).

Unsolved

Scientists love to solve problems, but a surprising number of mysteries have still not been fully explained... Read on, and find out more!

A mystery is a problem that we haven't yet solved.

Test your wits!

On the following pages, **Vital statistics** boxes give details of our Top 10 Spooky Mysteries. Each box contains a probable explanation, printed upside down. Try to solve the mystery yourself before reading the explanation.

So many reasons! So many mysteries!

They test our knowledge.

Mysterious world

There are mysteries everywhere. Some are new; some are thousands of years old. Some have been explained; others are still puzzling us. And beware: some mysteries are hoaxes!

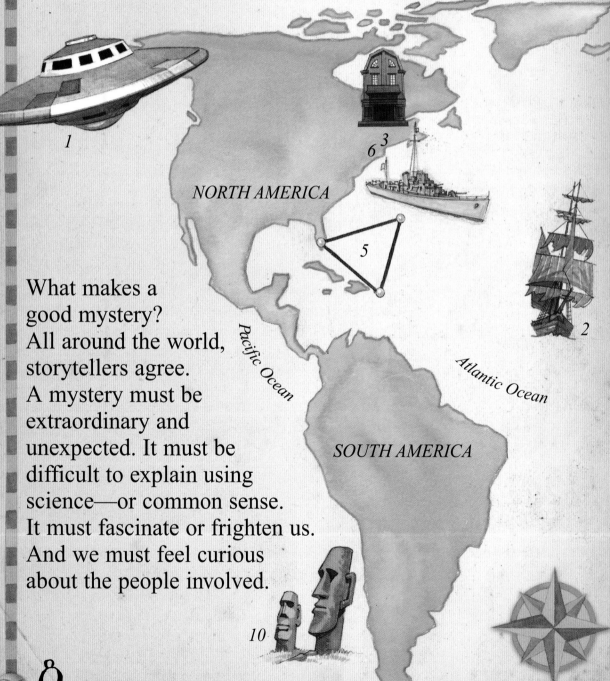

1

NORTH AMERICA

6 3

5

2

Pacific Ocean

Atlantic Ocean

SOUTH AMERICA

10

What makes a good mystery? All around the world, storytellers agree. A mystery must be extraordinary and unexpected. It must be difficult to explain using science—or common sense. It must fascinate or frighten us. And we must feel curious about the people involved.

1. *Alien invaders*
2. *The* Mary Celeste
3. *House of horror*
4. *The mummy's curse*
5. *Stormy waters*
6. *Invisible!*
7. *Wild child*
8. *Deadly dancing*
9. *Bodies in the snow*
10. *Lonely giants*

Out of this world

There are other mysterious places that never existed, such as El Dorado (South America), Atlantis (under the ocean) and Shangri-La (in the Himalayas). Their stories belong to an imaginary world.

EUROPE

7

8

9

4

ASIA

AFRICA

Explorers never found the kingdom of El Dorado.

It was named after me, the mysterious Golden Man!

AUSTRALIA

Strange but true

The mysteries in this book are all linked to real locations. Something strange actually happened at those places—even if we don't always know what it was!

9

№ 10

Lonely giants

The year is 1722. The place, the Pacific Ocean. Nervously, Dutch sailors scramble ashore—the first Europeans to reach the island. But stop! What's that? Who are they? Rows of huge stone giants line the shore, towering above them. All around is bleak wasteland with no trees.

We're Moai (honored ancestors). There are 887 of us.

Who built them? How? What for?

Vital statistics

Name: Rapa Nui (Easter Island)

Place: Pacific Ocean, 2,300 miles (3,700 km) west of Chile

Date: *c.*1600–1800

Mystery: Collapse of civilization, death of inhabitants

Probable explanation: Environmental disaster caused by cutting down trees.

You wouldn't want to know this:

The Easter Islanders grew so hungry that they fought—and ate—each other.

Kon-Tiki

In 1947, Norwegian adventurer Thor Heyerdahl sailed his raft *Kon-Tiki* from South America to one of the islands near Easter Island. He thought that the islands' first settlers had arrived that way—but scientists now believe this is unlikely.

Be prepared!
Always expect the very worst

"You won't believe this!"

Dreadful discoveries

Archaeologists on Easter Island have found carvings of starving people—and bones of butchered humans! But they can't decipher Rongorongo, the old Easter Island script—that's still a mystery.

Big bang!

In 1908, Siberia in northern Russia was blasted by a mysterious meteorite (or perhaps a comet). With a vivid blue flash and a noise like gunfire, it flattened 80 million trees and created 830 square miles (2,150 sq km) of desert.

Crack!

No trees, no food!

Trees gave the islanders timber for boat-building, and tree roots stopped soil from blowing away. But once the trees had been cut down, the islanders could not go fishing or grow food—so they went hungry.

Without water

The Nazca people of South America were amazing artists, creating giant pictures in the stony ground (left). But, around A.D. 700, their artistic efforts ended. Why? What happened? Droughts, and wars over water, made families flee Nazca lands.

11

Some Nazca pictures are almost 660 feet (200 m) long.

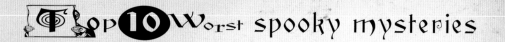

No 9

Bodies in the snow

It's bitterly cold, and you've joined a rescue party searching for nine young student skiers who have mysteriously disappeared. Ah! There's their tent, but it's ripped open! And way over there are partly clothed bodies (with burned hands!), frozen to death as they crawled through the snow. Later, you learn that more bodies have been found, with horrific injuries—a smashed skull, crushed ribs, and a missing tongue.

Vital statistics

Name: Dyatlov Pass incident
Place: A pass (lower slope between high peaks) in the Ural Mountains, Russia
Date: 1959
Mystery: Violent death of nine young skiers
Probable explanation: Maybe an avalanche, but no one knows for sure.

You wouldn't want to know this:

The students' dead bodies were said to have turned bright orange. Their hair had gone gray overnight. The night the students died, strange flashing lights were seen in the sky.

The temperature at Dyatlov Pass was way below freezing: -13°F (-25°C) or lower.

Be prepared!
Always expect the very worst

Murdered by a Monster?

Traditional tales told of huge, hairy monsters that lurked in the mountains. Had one of these wild giants killed the skiers? Probably not—there were no monster footprints. Hypothermia is more likely.

Cold kills!

Look out for these signs of hypothermia (dangerously low body temperature):

- Shivering, goose bumps
- Numb hands and feet
- Sickness, blurred vision
- Feeling strangely warm
- Clumsiness and confusion
- Violent shaking, very pale
- Dazed, then unconscious—death follows.

Danger zone

When examined after death, the skiers' clothes showed high levels of atomic radiation. Had they strayed into a deadly secret weapon-testing zone?

Boom!

Deadly rays!

Innocent explanation

Mutilated bodies are always mysterious and disturbing. When dead cattle with missing tongues were found in the United States around 1960, farmers blamed spacemen, or vandals. In fact, the soft flesh had been eaten by scavenging birds and animals.

No 8

Deadly dancing

Here we go! Here we go! Here we go! Look, here come the dancers—wild, bloodstained, exhausted. Respectable men, women, and children, dancing through the city streets. Yes, dancing until they drop dead! It's some sort of mass panic, caused by the troubled times they live in. They fear disease and war and famine, and feel very guilty for their sins.

Vital statistics

Name: Dancing plague
Place: Europe
Date: Around 1400–1600
Mystery: Why dance to death?

Probable explanation: Mass panic.

You wouldn't want to know this:

Dancers leaped and swayed until their feet were raw and bloody, then ran around like wild beasts.

I'm doomed!

Our world is coming to an end!

My feet are killing me.

Be prepared!
Always expect the very worst

Poison fungus on grain

Mass panic

Deadly diseases, such as bubonic plague, caused panic. Fearing sudden death, victims ran wild, collapsed, or became hysterical. Natural poisons also caused strange symptoms—scary visions, twitching limbs – but rarely led to dancing.

Meow!

Hisss!

Aaargh!

Bubo (deadly plague swelling)

No, Sister!

In the past, many Europeans believed in witchcraft and magic. This sometimes led to very strange behavior—even among good, holy people. In 1491, Spanish nuns began to crawl and climb like cats, believing that they had been possessed (taken over) by devils.

And all because of little old me!

Dance – and disappear!

Traditional tales tell how the Pied Piper of Hamelin saved the citizens from a plague of rats in 1284. When they would not pay him, he played his pipe again. This time, all the town's children (*except two) danced after him into a mysterious cave. They were never seen again.

*Some say that only one was left.

15

No 7

Wild child

Poor Victor! His life was tragic. No one knew where he came from, but one day he was found in the woods, eating roots and acorns. About 12 years old, he had no clothes and was filthy dirty. He could not talk, but sniffed at his captors like a dog. They took him to the big city, where experts tried—and mostly failed—to teach him "civilized" behavior. He died at just 40 years old.

Vital statistics

Name: Victor, the Wild Boy of Aveyron
Place: France
Date: 1800
Mystery: Boy living wild in the woods

Probable explanation: Victor had mental problems, and had been abandoned (to die) by adults.

You wouldn't want to know this:

Like any other wild creature, Victor was not house-trained. Slowly, he had to learn to use a lavatory.

Be prepared!
Always expect the very worst

fierce but famous

Legend has it that Romulus and Remus were nursed by a wolf, and grew up fierce and quarrelsome, like wild beasts. They built a great city, but Romulus killed Remus. Today, the city (Rome, the capital of Italy) is still named after him.

Better than human?

In *The Jungle Book* (1894), British writer Rudyard Kipling told stories about a wild boy in the Indian jungle and his animal friends. Most of Kipling's creatures were kinder and wiser than humans.

Angels or devils?

Around 1800, scholars wanted to study children's behavior. Some said that children were naturally wild, like Victor. Others said children were born good, but learned to be bad by copying adults around them.

I wonder who was right...

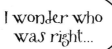

The horrible truth

In real life, wild animals are not nice to children. That's why traditional tales like "Little Red Riding Hood" were invented. Such stories warn children not to stray into wild places, or they'll meet with deadly danger.

All the better to EAT you with, my dear!

17

No 6

Invisible!

Just imagine! It's wartime, and you're in a U.S. Navy dockyard. There's a small ship next to you —the USS *Eldridge*—and suddenly it disappears in a flash of weird light! Ten seconds *earlier*, it slowly comes back. Some of the crew are welded to its hull, some have gone mad with fear. Others have vanished!

Vital statistics

Name: The Philadelphia Experiment
Date: 1943
Place: Philadelphia, Pennsylvania, U.S.
Mystery: Strange science: an invisible ship

Probable explanation: Wartime worries; crazy story.

You wouldn't want to know this:

At the time when the "Philadelphia Experiment" story was created, many people feared that new, scientific weapons would soon blow the world to bits.

Be prepared!
Always expect the very worst

Science fiction

In 1957, scribbled notes arrived at U.S. Navy headquarters. The writer claimed that scientists had been trying to make the USS *Eldridge* invisible—but, because the experiment had gone wrong, it had been kept top secret. The story was completely untrue—but millions believed it!

Changing waves

In naval dockyards like the one at Philadelphia, warships were electrically treated so that underwater mines could not detect them. This changed the pattern of magnetic waves around the ships' hulls. But they did not disappear!

These are strange orders, Captain! First we turn to green fog, then we disappear!

Einstein's ideas

Albert Einstein (1879–1955) was the greatest scientist of the 20th century. His theories suggest that it might be possible to distort (bend or stretch) space, light, and time. Perhaps they inspired the story?

Military mysteries

Although there was no Philadephia Experiment, the U.S. Army did investigate strange science. For example, in the 1970s, soldiers tried to use mind power to kill. They practiced by staring at goats!

$E = mc^2$

I surrender!

19

No 5

Stormy waters

You've probably heard of it—the famous Bermuda Triangle. Hundreds of ships and planes are rumored to have vanished there, without warning, very mysteriously!

But in 1975, careful calculations proved that there were no more shipwrecks or plane crashes there than in any other busy transport zone.

United States

Bermuda

Florida

Puerto Rico

Caribbean Sea

Vital statistics

Name: Bermuda Triangle
Date: 1945–1975
Place: Sea between southeastern U.S. and Bermuda
Mystery: Disappearing ships and planes

Probable explanation: Imagined by journalists, who wanted to sell exciting stories.

You wouldn't want to know this:

The Bermuda Triangle was also known as the Devil's Triangle. That was meant to show how scary it was!

The real mystery is why people still say the Bermuda Triangle is dangerous!

Don't spoil it! We all like a good story!

Be prepared!
Always expect the very worst

Alien attack?

The Bermuda Triangle was first mentioned in stories about the doomed Flight 19: in 1945, five U.S. Navy planes vanished mysteriously. Probably, their pilots made a fatal mistake and crashed into the sea—but some writers blamed space invaders.

Natural hazards?

Other writers said that hurricanes, wild waves, fast currents, and giant bubbles of natural gas from the seabed had wrecked ships sailing across the Bermuda Triangle. This was possible, but could not be proved.

Hurricanes often strike Bermuda.

Whoosh!

Into the unknown?

Disappearances have always made good stories. In A.D. 117, it was said, the Roman Ninth Legion marched out of York, England, and vanished! In fact, the legion really was overpowered by enemies—but that happened 15 years later, and in the Middle East!

Why *let* facts spoil a good story?

Roar!

Does it really matter who destroyed us?

21

No 4

The mummy's curse

The magnificent golden treasures found in Pharaoh Tutankhamun's tomb caused a worldwide sensation when they were discovered in 1922. The death soon after of Lord Carnarvon, who had paid for the excavations, became almost as famous. People linked the two events, and declared: "A mysterious curse killed him!"

Vital statistics

Name: Curse of Tutankhamun
Date: 1922 onwards
Place: Valley of the Kings, Egypt
Mystery: Did an ancient curse kill archaeologists who discovered Tutankhamun's tomb?

Probable solution Lord Carnarvon's death was a coincidence—the curse was just an exotic, exciting rumor!

You wouldn't want to know this:

Deadly bacteria and poisonous gases are often found in ancient tombs—even today.

Can you see anything?

Wonderful things!

22

Be prepared!
Always expect the very worst

Unlucky treasures?

Great wealth made onlookers envious. Sometimes they may have felt like cursing the rich. But many curses were invented—by merchants selling treasures. A story of a mysterious curse brought publicity, raised prices, and added a thrill to business deals.

Since 1908, it's been claimed that the beautiful blue Hope Diamond is cursed and brings disaster. Today's value? $250 million!

Life after death

Magic spells and religious sayings decorated the entrance to many Egyptian tombs. But they were not curses. Most were designed to help dead people survive for ever in the afterlife.

The real reason

There was no curse! Lord Carnarvon had been in poor health for many years. He died from a mosquito bite that became infected and poisoned him.

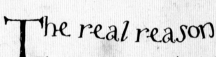

How, why, who?

Mighty, mysterious, and very, very old, the pyramids in Egypt puzzled people for centuries. Some said aliens built them, or a vanished superhuman race. Actually, Egypt's farmers built the pyramids, using muscle power and simple tools of stone and copper.

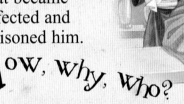

Now that *is* amazing.

23

House of horror

Tourists flocked to Amityville to see the mysterious house of horror.

First, it was a house of tragedy. In 1974, a young man living there murdered his parents, brothers, and sisters. A year later, a new family moved in—but fled in terror just 28 days later. They claimed they were driven out by horrific ghosts and demons. Was the house evil and haunted, as they said? Or had they imagined everything— then sought publicity for their story?

> Do you get the feeling it's looking at us?

Vital statistics

Name: House of horror
Place: Amityville, Long Island, New York, U.S.
Date: 1975
Mystery: Ghastly haunted house

Probable explanation: A hoax.

You wouldn't want to know this:

It was said that the youngest child of the new arrivals at Amityville was haunted by an evil, pig-faced monster!

Be prepared!
Always expect the very worst

Very, very nasty

The new family claimed to be pestered by strange sounds, vile smells, swarms of flies, and sickly green slime. They spoke of red staring eyes in the darkness, demon footprints, and much more. A best-selling book and nine films were based on their story.

Unquiet spirits?

Had mysterious ghosts led the young man to murder, and then haunted the new family? Was the Amityville house built on an old site, where Native Americans once died? Absolutely not—although some people thought so. History shows that no such place existed.

Oddly enough, I slept through some of these horrors. Sometimes I wonder if they really happened...

Who's next for the Ripper?

Worse than human?

In 1888, London was shocked by a series of brutal murders. The killer was never discovered, but was nicknamed "Jack the Ripper." Some said that he was not a man, but a monster. Like tourists at Amityville, who believed in demons, they did not like to think that humans could be so evil.

Nº 2

The Mary Celeste

Ship ahoy! There she is! It's the *Mary Celeste*, sailing through calm seas with her heavy, dangerous cargo. But hey, that's strange! She's not steering straight, and her sails are flapping wildly. I can't see anyone on deck. It looks as though they've all abandoned her!

> She's carrying barrels of alcohol.

> You have to be careful with that. It can explode.

Vital statistics

Name: *Mary Celeste*
Date: 1872
Place: Atlantic Ocean, near Portugal
Mystery: Empty ship, no sign of crew

Probable explanation: The crew abandoned ship because they feared sinking, or an explosion.

You wouldn't want to know this:

The captain's two-year-old daughter was on board. She vanished along with the others.

Be prepared! Always expect the very worst

Whoooosh!

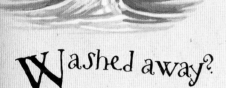

Washed away?

Rescuers found water more than 3 feet (1 m) deep in the *Mary Celeste*'s hold. Above, everything was soaking wet, from the captain's bed to the ship's compass. Was the ship swamped by freak waves or a whirling waterspout? No one knows!

The flying Dutchman

Another sea mystery! Many sailors claim to have seen this ghostly ship and its haunted captain. They're always a warning of bad luck and foul weather. The *Flying Dutchman* appears suddenly, bathed in an eerie glow. Its story may perhaps be based on real-life mirages.

I'm doomed! My punishment is to sail the seas forever!

A watery grave?

No one knows what happened to the *Mary Celeste*'s sailors. Without witnesses or evidence, their fate remains a mystery. Probably, they climbed overboard into the lifeboat. Then they either died of cold, of hunger and thirst, or drowned.

We're safer here. That ship's dangerous!

No 1

Alien invaders

Tall and green? Short and silver? Friendly, peculiar, dangerous? Who knows what alien invaders might look like? Except in films, on TV, and in computer games, no one has ever seen one. Unless, perhaps, you believe the mysterious stories told about a ranch at Roswell, New Mexico. There, a farmhand thought he might have found strange wreckage—from a spaceship!

Vital statistics

Name: The Roswell Incident
Date: 1947
Place: Roswell, New Mexico, U.S.
Mystery: Did an alien spacecraft crash-land here?

Probable explanation: The U.S. Army was testing secret equipment.

You wouldn't want to know this:

Some say that mangled bodies of space invaders were found close to the crash at Roswell. One was still alive, and possibly dangerous…

Be prepared!
Always expect the very worst

flying saucer?

A mysterious tangle of rubber and tinfoil was found at the Roswell ranch. Was it part of a flying saucer—or, as Army experts insisted, only the remains of a secret spy balloon that had been tracking enemy weapons?

foo fighters

In the 1940s, calm, trained, professional pilots saw mysterious balls of light that glowed bright, raced through the sky, and disappeared. Nicknamed "foo fighters," they have never been fully explained. They may have been rocket flares, or a kind of lightning.

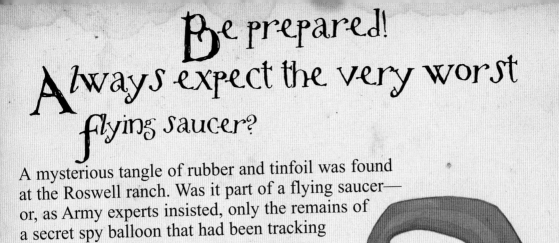

A tragic end?

The mysterious Roswell "aliens" may have been dummies, used by aircraft designers to measure the impact of crash-landings. Or, tragically, they may have been the crew of a U.S. Air Force plane, killed when its fuel tanks exploded.

Humans? No, I don't believe in them.

29

Glossary

Ancestor A grandparent, great-grandparent, etc.

Archaeologist A scientist who studies the remains of past civilizations.

Atlantis An imaginary land which is said to have sunk into the sea thousands of years ago.

Avalanche A sudden fall of ice, snow or rocks down a hillside.

Bacteria Tiny living things which can only be seen with a microscope. Some of them can cause disease.

Bubo A painful swelling that is a sign of bubonic plague.

Bubonic plague A disease that killed millions of people in medieval Europe. It is spread by diseased fleas that live on rats.

Comet An object that orbits the sun and has a glowing "tail" behind it.

Drought A lack of water.

El Dorado An imaginary land in South America, said to be very rich. Its name means "the Golden One."

Environmental disaster Serious damage to the natural world, caused by humans. Deforestation (destroying forests by cutting down trees) is an example.

Excavation The process of digging into the ground to look for remains of past civilizations.

Famine A great shortage of food.

Hoax A trick or practical joke.

Hold The part of a ship where cargo is stored.

Hurricane A storm with strong winds and heavy rain.

Hypothermia Low body temperature, which can cause death.

Hysterical Emotionally excited or disturbed.

Legion A regiment of the ancient Roman army.

Meteorite A piece of rock from space that has fallen to Earth.

Mine An underwater bomb.

Moai A statue of an ancestor on Rapa Nui (Easter Island).

Mutilated Badly damaged.

Pass A passage between two mountains.

Pharaoh The title of the king of ancient Egypt.

Possessed Taken over by demons or evil spirits.

Scavenging Living on dead animals or on food left behind by other animals.

Script An alphabet or method of writing.

Shangri-La An imaginary place in the Himalayas, where life is said to be happy and peaceful all the time.

Teleported (in science fiction) Instantly transported from one place to another.

USS United States Ship – a title given to ships of the U.S. Navy.

Waterspout A tornado (whirlwind) at sea.

Index